Hometowns

We are all members of a community.

SCHOLASTIC

LITERACY PLACE®

Copyright acknowledgments and credit appear on page 160, which constitutes an extension of this copyright page.

Copyright © 1996 by Scholastic Inc.　　　　All rights reserved.　　　　Printed in the U.S.A.

ISBN 0-590-49158-X

6 7 8 9 10　　　　　　23　　　　　　02 01 00 99 98

Come
to a Mayor's Office

We are all members
of a community.

People and Places

A community is made up of people and places.

Pitch In

We make our community a better place.

5

Helping Others

People in a community help each other.

Trade Books

The following books accompany this *Hometowns* SourceBook.

Fiction
Michael Bird-Boy
by Tomie dePaola

Chapter Book
Fox on Wheels
by Edward Marshall
illustrated by
James Marshall

Realistic Fiction
The Leaving Morning
by Angela Johnson
illustrated by David Soman

Big Books

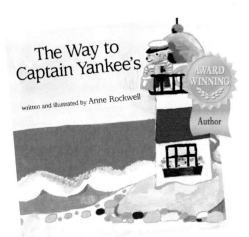

Fiction
The Way to Captain Yankee's
by Anne Rockwell

Realistic Fiction
Margaret and Margarita
by Lynn Reiser

8

People and Places

A community is made up of people and places.

Meet all the people who use a park bench in a very busy city.

Meet the mayor of Hilo, Hawaii. See what's the same and what's different about his town and the town where you live.

Learn why maps are made and how they are used. Meet children who painted a map on their school playground.

The Park Bench

Fumiko Takeshita • Mamoru Suzuki

The day has just begun.
A white mist hangs over the park.
No one is here yet, and the park is very still.
Under a tree sits a single white park bench.

こうえんの　あさ。
きりが　しろい。みずも　しろい。
まだ　だれも　こない　こうえんは,
とても　しずか。
きの　したに,　しろい　ベンチが　ひとつ。

こうえんに　いちばんのりは，はやおきの　ひと。
たいそうを　する　ひと。いぬを　つれた　ひと。
しろい　ベンチも　めを　さます。
あ，いつもの　おじさんが，ちいさな　くるまで　やって。

The early risers are the first to arrive.

Some do exercises. Others walk their dogs.

The white bench is just now waking up.

Look, here comes the park worker in his little motor cart.

13

"Good morning, my dear park bench,"
says the worker. "It's cleaning day for the
park," and he gives the bench a friendly
little pat.

Children pass by on their way to school.
Adults pass by on their way to work.
The town is becoming lively.

「やあ，おはよう，しろい　ベンチ。
きょうは，こうえんを
きれいに　する　ひだよ。」
ベンチを　ぽんと　たたいて，
おじさんは，しごとを　はじめる。

がっこうに　いく　ひとが　とおる。
かいしゃに　いく　ひとが　とおる。
まちが　にぎやかに　なって　くる。

こうえんに，おじいさんが さんぽに きた。
つえを ついて ゆっくり。
はなを みたり，とりを みたり，
いそがないで ゆっくり。

「やれやれ，どっこいしょ。」
しろい ベンチで ひとやすみ。
「ちょうど いい ところに，
ちょうど いい ベンチが あるね。」

Here comes an old man
taking his walk.
He moves very slowly,
leaning on his cane.
He stops to smell the flowers
and then to feed the birds.
He's not in any hurry.

"Now it's time for a rest,"
says the old man.
He sits on the white bench.
"The perfect bench in just
the right place," he thinks.

Along comes a mother and her baby.
"Let's sit in the sun," she says.
"The white bench is bathed in sunlight."

"Da, da," the baby babbles.
"Goo, goo," the old man replies.
What *can* they be talking about?

つぎに　きたのは，あかちゃんと　おかあさん。
「ひなたぼっこしましょ。
しろい　ベンチに　おひさまが　いっぱい。」

ばあ，ばあって　あかちゃん。
ほう，ほうって　おじいさん。
ふたりで　なんの　おはなしして　いるの？

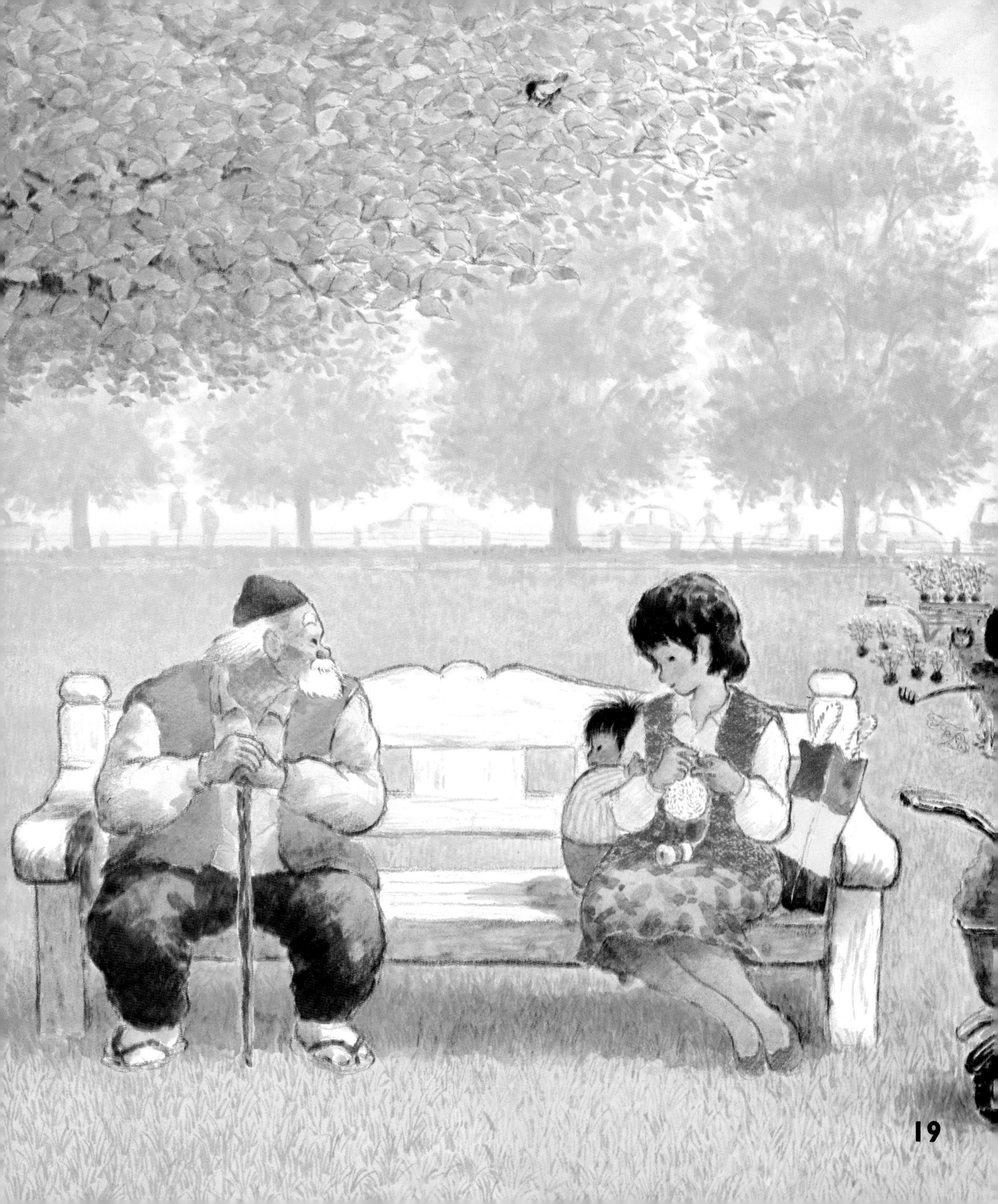

Friends meet at the park.
The two mothers begin to chat.
They talk on and on.
Chitter-chatter, chitter-chatter, until it's time to eat.

All the while the white bench listens quietly.

こうえんで　であったら,
すぐに　おしゃべり　ぺちゃくちゃ。
いつに　なっても　おわらない。
おなかが　すくまで　ぺちゃくちゃ　ぺちゃくちゃ。

だまって　きいて　いる　しろい　ベンチ。

It's lunch time. The park worker eats under a large tree.
Here come the cats and the birds.
"Okay, my little friends. I'll give you some food," he says.
"But, oops, don't make the bench dirty."

こうえんの　きの　したで,

おじさんの　おひる。

ほら，あつまって　きた

のらねこたち，ことりたち。

「よしよし，いま　わけて　やるからな。

おっと，ベンチを　よごさないで　くれよ。」

ひるやすみの　こうえん。いろんな　ひとが　くる。
「ひるねには　やっぱり，この　ベンチが　いちばん　いいや。」
ふんわり　そよかぜが　いい　きもち。
ベンチも　いっしょに　うっとりする。

During the noon hour, lots of people come to the park to relax.

"This park bench is my favorite spot for a nap," says a man.

A gentle breeze is blowing, and the park bench begins

to feel drowsy, too.

26

A young man waits for his friend who is late.
"Let's meet in the park, at the white bench,"
they had agreed. "But now, where can she be?"

("Wait, who left a book on the bench?"
the park worker wonders.)

「こうえんで　あおうね。

いつもの　しろい　ベンチでね。」って

やくそくしたのに，なかなか　こない　ともだち。

やくそく　わすれて　いないかなあ。

（おや，ベンチの　うえに　だれかの　わすれもの。）

Here comes a group of children running to the park.
This is the liveliest time of day.
"What are we going to play today?" asks one child.
"Let's talk it over."

こどもたちが　おおぜい　やって　きた。

こうえんが　いちばん　にぎやかに　なる　じかん。

「きょうは，なに　して　あそぶ？」

「そうだんしよう。しろい　ベンチに

みんな　あつまれー！」

29

しろい　ベンチは，おうちに　なる。おしろに　なる。

しまに　なる。ふねに　なる。でんしゃに　なる。

えきに　なる。　それから　ベンチにも　なる。

All of a sudden the white bench becomes a house.

Now it's a castle, then an island, now a boat.

Now a train. Then a station.

And then, it's even a park bench again!

Plip plop, plip plop . . .
"Uh-oh, here it comes," says the worker to himself.

Suddenly, it begins to rain. Everyone runs for shelter.
Everyone except, of course, the white bench.

ぽつん，ぽつん，ぱららん……。
「おっ，ふって　きたかな。」

あめ，あめ，にわかあめ。
はしって，はしって，あまやどり。
きが　ぬれる。しばふが　ぬれる。
しろい　ベンチも　あめの　なか。

The rain has stopped.
Now the sky is bright.
The wet flowers and grass glisten.
"You're soaking wet," says the park worker
to the bench, as he gently wipes it dry.
"You're a fine bench in spite of your age," he says.
"I know you'll last for a long, long time."

あめが　やんだ。　まぶしい　そら。

はなにも，　くさにも，

ひかる　しずくが　いっぱい。

「おやおや，　びしょぬれだ。」

おじさんが　ベンチを　ふいて　くれたよ。

「ずいぶん　ふるく　なったけど，

いい　ベンチだからなあ。

まだまだ　がんばって　くれよ。」

こうえんの ゆうぐれ。ちょっぴり かぜが つめたく なる。
「また あしたね。」って てを ふって,
こどもたちが かえって いく。
しろい ベンチも ゆうぐれの いろ。

Now the day is ending.

The air becomes chilly.

Children wave to each other as they leave for home.

The white park bench is perfectly still in the twilight.

When the lights go on in the town,
the worker's day is done.
"Good night, my dear white bench,"
he says. "You must be very tired.
I'll see you tomorrow."
He turns on the lights of his little
motor cart and drives home.

まちに　あかりが　ともる　ころ,
おじさんの　しごとも　おしまいだ。
「さよなら,　しろい　ベンチ。
きょうも　いちにち　おつかれさま。
じゃ,　また　くるよ。」
ちいさな　くるまに　ライトを　つけて,
おじさんが　かえって　いく。

The park is covered with darkness.
Stars twinkle in the sky.
No one is here now, and the park is very still.
Under a tree sits a single white park bench.

Good night.

こうえんの　よる。
そらに　ほしが　きらり　きらり。
もう　だれも　いない　こうえんは，
とても　しずか。
きの　したに，しろい　ベンチが　ひとつ。

おやすみなさい。

MENTOR

 Read Together!

Steve Yamashiro

Mayor

Steve Yamashiro is the mayor of Hilo, Hawaii. A mayor makes sure everybody is safe and can enjoy the town they live in.

Mayor Yamashiro does his paperwork and has meetings in his office.

As mayor, Steve Yamashiro spends time with people who live in his town.

"The best thing about being mayor is I work with many people," says Steve Yamashiro. "We make changes for everyone who lives here."

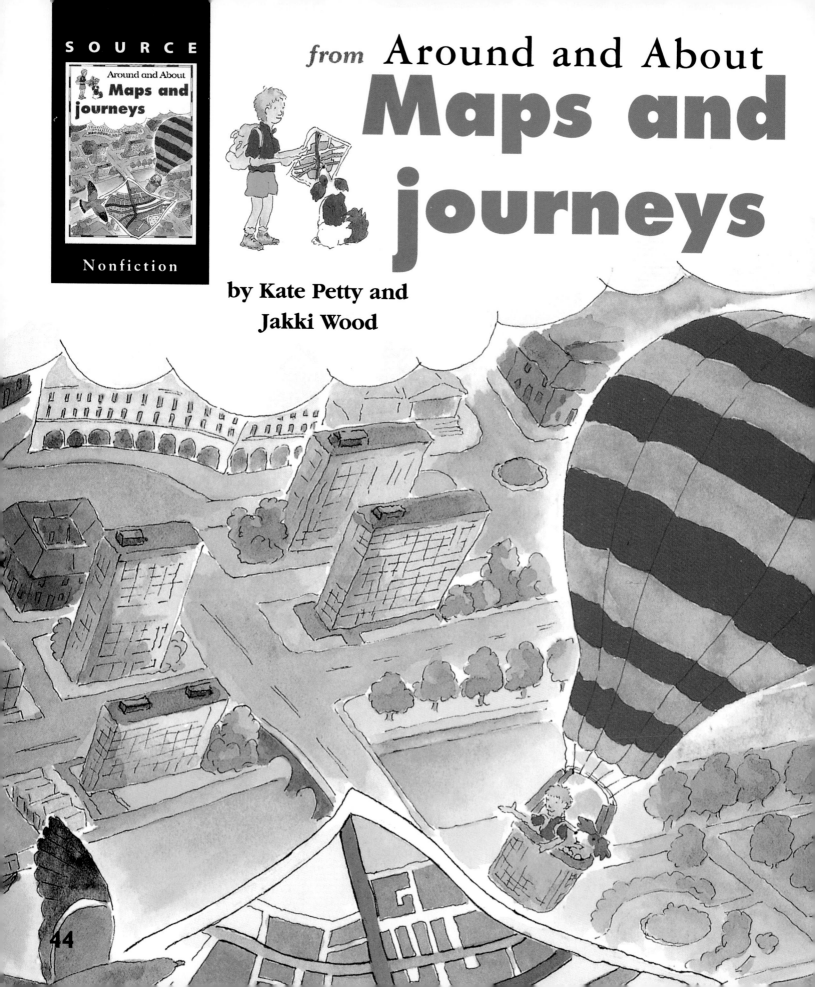

from Around and About
Maps and
journeys

by Kate Petty and
Jakki Wood

44

Don't get lost

Meet Harry and his dog, Ralph.
They like to travel all over the place.
Harry wants to find his way around
without getting lost, so he's going to
learn about maps.

A view from above

When Harry and Ralph walk along
the street, they can't see what's around the
corner. But when they look down from a
balloon, they can see everything laid out.
They can see the church and
the station and all the
roads in between.

A map or a plan of a place is like the view from above.

Drawing a plan

Harry and Ralph decide to make a plan of the garden. They can see its shape from above.

I've got a piece of paper.

I've got a pencil .. let's land.

Harry walks from the front of the garden to the back. It is 30 steps long. Then he walks from one side to the other. It is 16 steps wide.

Harry draws his steps on the paper. Now he wants to put in the rose tree and the pond. How can he find out exactly where to put them?

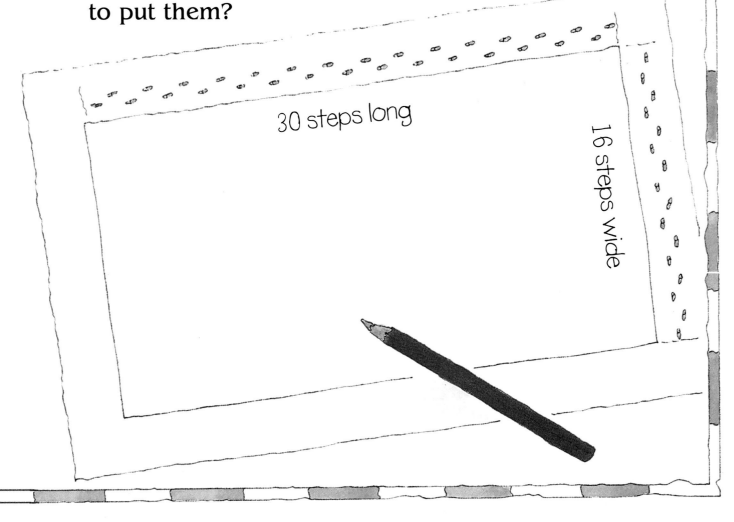

30 steps long

16 steps wide

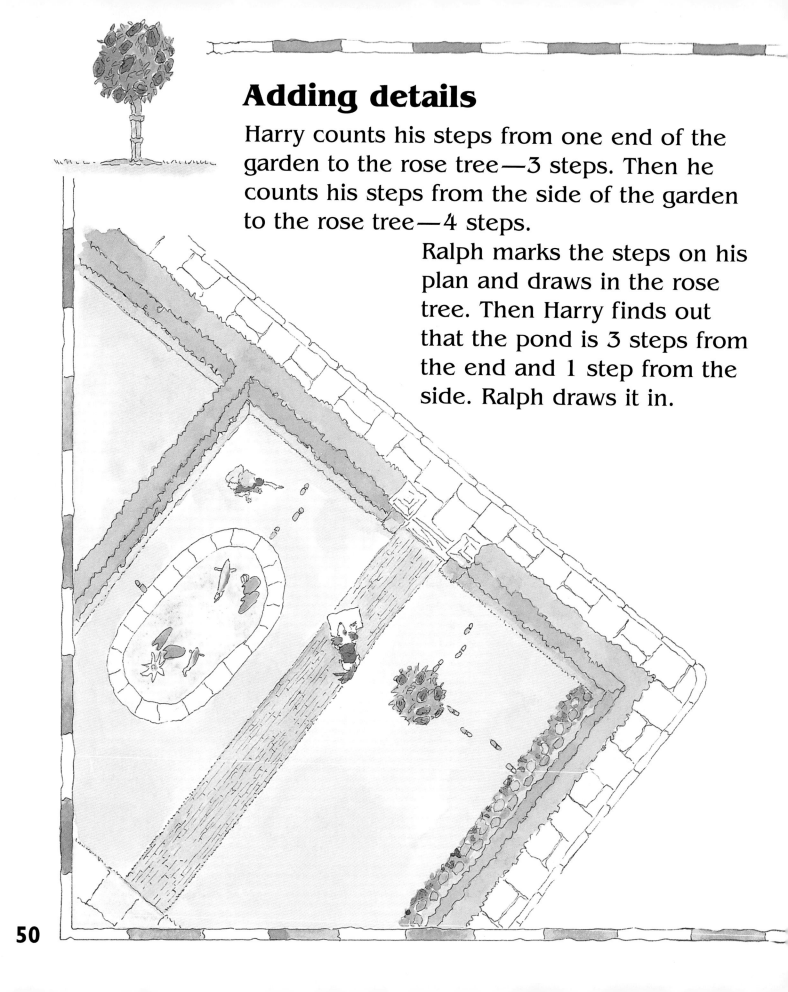

Adding details

Harry counts his steps from one end of the garden to the rose tree—3 steps. Then he counts his steps from the side of the garden to the rose tree—4 steps.

Ralph marks the steps on his plan and draws in the rose tree. Then Harry finds out that the pond is 3 steps from the end and 1 step from the side. Ralph draws it in.

Ralph measures the garden with a tape measure. It is 60 feet (18 meters) long, which means that one of Harry's steps is 2 feet (0.6 meter) long. They draw a scale on their plan. Make a plan of your garden or your classroom.

2 feet

The route to school

Look at the picture opposite. It shows Harry's school at the top, the church in the middle, and Harry's house at the bottom. Below, Harry is making a map of his way, or route, to school. He thinks hard about where he turns left and where he turns right. He draws in landmarks, which are special things like the bridge and the church that he sees on the way. He marks in his route.

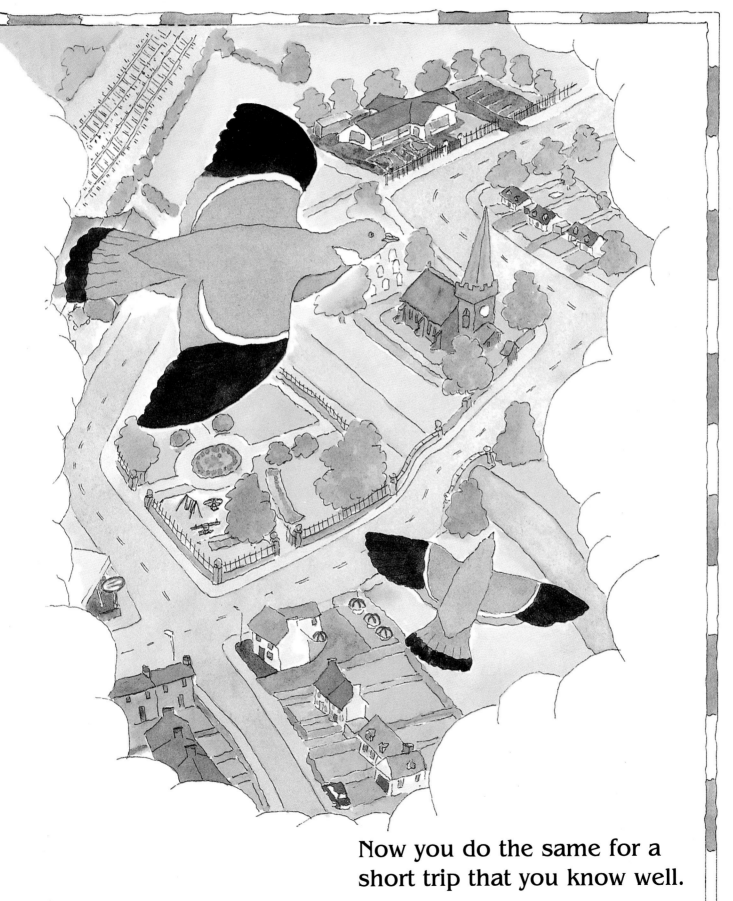

Now you do the same for a
short trip that you know well.

SOURCE
KidCity®
Magazine

The World's

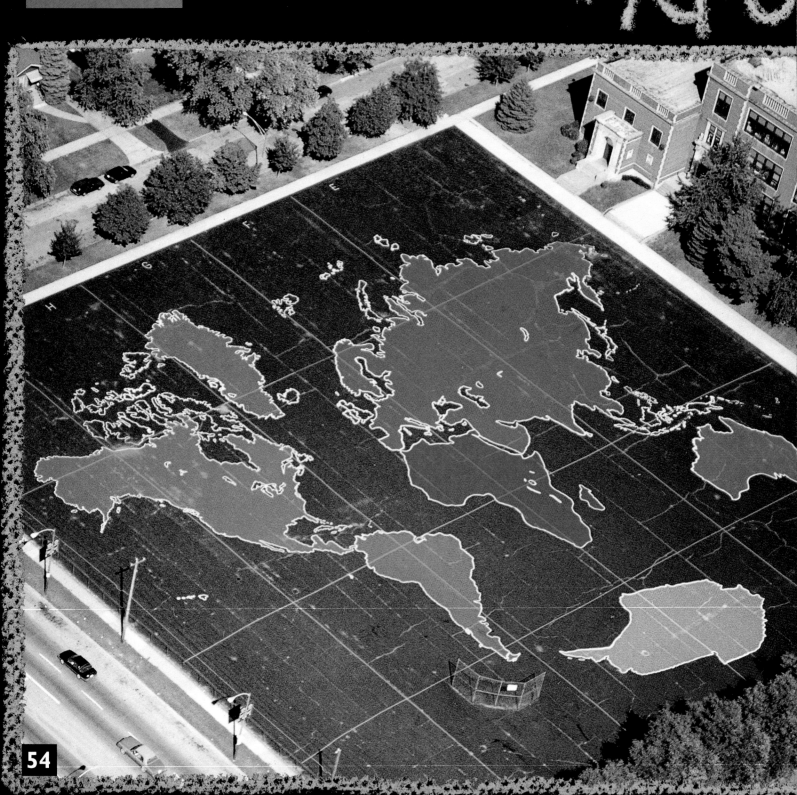

a playground

Chicago, IL—When kids at Clissold Elementary need to check a map, they can just look out their school window. About 40 kids and grown-ups painted what may be one of the largest maps of the world right on the cement at their playground.

The kids first sketched out chalk lines, looked at lots of other maps as guides, and then carefully used a small paint machine. Only the outlines of the continents and waterways were finished with permanent paint. The rest was filled in by students with colored chalk.

Read Together!

Pitch In

We make our community a better place.

Join Henry and Mudge as they learn a lesson about the environment. Then read an old poem that says a lot to us today.

Read a folk tale that tells how two tricksters get a town to share with each other.

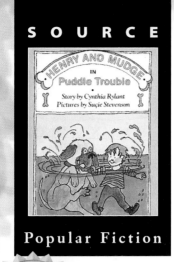

from

The Snow Glory

Story by Cynthia Rylant
Pictures by Suçie Stevenson

When the snow melted
and Spring came,
Henry and his dog Mudge
stayed outside
all the time.

Henry had missed
riding his bike.
Mudge had missed
chewing on sticks.
They were glad
it was warmer.

One day when Henry and Mudge
were in their yard,
Henry saw something blue
on the ground.
He got closer to it.
"Mudge," he called.
"It's a flower!"
Mudge slowly walked over
and sniffed the blue flower.

Then he sneezed
all over Henry.
"Aw, Mudge," Henry said.

Later, Henry's mother
told him that the flower
was called a snow glory.
"Can I pick it?"
Henry asked.
"Oh, no," said his mother.
"Let it grow."
So Henry didn't pick it.

Every day he saw the snow glory
in the yard,
blue
and looking so pretty.
He knew he shouldn't pick it.
He was trying not to pick it.
But he thought how nice
it would look in a jar.
He thought how nice
to bring it inside.
He thought how nice
it would be
to own that snow glory.
Every day he stood with Mudge
and looked at the flower.

Mudge would stick his nose
into the grass
all around the snow glory.
But he never looked at it
the way Henry did.
"Don't you think the snow glory
has been growing long enough?"
Henry would ask his mother.
"Let it grow, Henry,"
she would say.

Oh, Henry wanted that snow glory.
And one day
he just knew
he had to have it.
So he took Mudge
by the collar
and he stood
beside the snow glory.

"I'm going to pick it,"
Henry whispered to Mudge.
"I've let it grow a long time."
Henry bent his head and
he said in Mudge's ear,
"Now I *need* it."
And Mudge wagged his tail,
licked Henry's face,
then put his big mouth
right over that snow glory . . .

and he ate it.
"*No, Mudge!*" Henry said.
But too late.
There was a blue flower
in Mudge's belly.

"I said *need* it, not *eat* it!"
shouted Henry.
He was so mad because
Mudge took his flower.
It was Henry's flower
and Mudge took it.

And Henry almost said,
"Bad dog," but he stopped.

He looked at Mudge,
who looked back at him
with soft brown eyes
and a flower in his belly.

Henry knew it wasn't his snow glory.

He knew it wasn't anybody's snow glory.

Just a thing to let grow.

And if someone ate it,

it was just a thing to let go.

Henry stopped feeling mad.

He put his arms around
Mudge's big head.

"Next time, Mudge,"
he said,
"try to *listen* better."
Mudge wagged his tail
and licked his lips.
One blue petal
fell from his mouth
into Henry's hand.
Henry smiled,
put it in his pocket,
and they went inside.

Hurt No Living Thing

by Christina Rossetti
illustrated by David Slonim

Hurt no living thing;
Ladybird, nor butterfly,
Nor moth with dusty wing,
Nor cricket chirping cheerily,
Nor grasshopper so light of leap,
Nor dancing gnat, nor beetle fat,
Nor harmless worms that creep.

Stone
Soup

a French folk tale retold
by Adrienne Betz
illustrated by John O'Brien

SCHOLASTIC

AWARD
WINNING
Illustrator

Once upon a time, a poor woman and her son were very far from home. Their names were Marie and Henri, and they had traveled a long, long way. They had no food. They were so hungry!

At last they came to a town. The travelers went from house to house and asked, "Friend, do you have a bit of food to spare?"

"No!" said the woman at the first house.

"No!" said the man at the second house.

"No!" said the little girl who peeked out from behind the door at the third house.

The hungry travelers asked the baker,
the tailor, and the shoemaker.

The baker said, "No!"

The tailor said, "No!"

The shoemaker said, "No!"

They even asked at the mayor's house,
and even the mayor said, "No, I have
nothing to share!"

"Mr. Mayor," said Henri. "Your town must be very poor! No one has as much as a crust of bread to share."

"But we will help you," said Marie. "We know a way to feed your whole town. All we need is a big pot. Do you have one?"

The mayor called to his children, "Bring out our big pot!"

He opened his door wide. The children came out carrying the BIGGEST pot the travelers had ever seen.

"Thank you, my friends!" said Marie.

MAYOR

The travelers carried the pot to the center of town.
Henri filled the pot with water. Marie built a fire
around the pot. Everyone in town came out to
watch them.

"Welcome, friends," said Marie. "Please, join us!
My dear son and I are going to make a very special
soup for you. It's called stone soup."

Then, as everyone watched, Marie bent down,
picked up a stone, and dropped it right into the pot.

The baker said, "Impossible!"

The tailor said, "Impossible!"

The shoemaker said, "Impossible!"

"No one can make soup from a stone!" said the mayor.

"Watch and learn, my friends," said Marie with a smile.

Then she took a big spoon out of her traveling bag. She used the spoon to stir the pot.

"Ah," said Henri. "There's nothing as good as stone soup! Of course, it would be even BETTER if we had a carrot. But where would we ever find one?"

"I think I know where to find a carrot!" said one woman.

"Thank you, my friend," Marie said. "This would be the perfect time to add carrots to the soup."

The woman raced home and came back
with a bunch of carrots.

Marie quickly sliced the carrots and stirred
them into the soup.

"Ah," said Henri. "There's nothing as good as stone soup! Of course, it would be even BETTER if we had a potato. But where would we ever find one?"

"I think I know where to find a potato!" said a man.

"Thank you, my friend," Marie said. "This would be the perfect time to add potatoes to the soup."

The man raced home and came back with a sack of potatoes.

Marie quickly sliced the potatoes and stirred them into the soup.

"Ah," said Henri, "there's nothing as good as stone soup! Of course, it would be even BETTER if we had a few beans. But where would we ever find some?"

"I'll bring some beans," said a little girl.

"I don't have any beans," said a little boy. "But I do have some cabbage!"

Now everyone in town thought of something that he or she could bring.

Marie quickly sliced and stirred all the good things into the soup. The soup was now so thick that it was hard to stir it.

"We can help," said the baker, the tailor, and the shoemaker. They all took turns stirring the pot.

At last the soup was ready!

Again everyone raced home. This time they came back with bowls and spoons. Marie used her big spoon to fill each bowl.

The mayor was the very first to try the soup. "Mmmmmm," said the mayor. "It's amazing! Soup from a stone!"

"Mmmmmmmm," said the townspeople. "It's amazing AND delicious!"

They all ate and ate until they could not eat any more. Then everyone sang songs and laughed together until the stars came out.

The mayor made a speech. "We all thank you!"
he said to Marie and Henri. "Please stay in our town
as long as you like!"

That night, the travelers went home with the
mayor and his family. They were given the finest
beds in the house.

"Ah," said Henri to his mother as she tucked him in.
"There's nothing as good as stone soup, ESPECIALLY
when you have friends to share it with you!"

Read Together!

Helping Others

People in a community help each other.

See how two very special friends make a special trade. Then read about some first graders who visit an old friend.

Discover how a whole village helps a girl take care of her younger brother.

A Special Trade

Sally Wittman

A Public Tele...
Story t...

Pictures by Karen Gundersheimer

AWARD
WINNING

Book

Old Bartholomew is Nelly's neighbor.

When Nelly was very small,
he would take her every day
for a walk down the block to
Mrs. Pringle's vegetable garden.

Bartholomew never pushed too fast.
He always warned Nelly about
Mr. Oliver's bumpy driveway:
"Hang on, Nell! Here's a bump!"
And she'd shout "BUMP!" as she rode over it.

If they met a nice dog along
the way, they'd stop and pet it.

But if it was nasty, Bartholomew
would shoo it away.

When Mrs. Pringle's sprinkler was on,
he would say, "Get ready, get set,
CHAAARRRRRRRRRRRRGE!"
Nelly would squeal "Wheeeee!"
as he pushed her through it.

When Nelly began to walk, Bartholomew took her by the hand. "NO-NO!" she cried, pulling it back. Nelly didn't want any help.

So Bartholomew offered his hand only when she really needed it.

Bartholomew was getting older, too. He needed a walking stick. So they walked very slowly. When they walked upstairs, they *both* held on to the railing.

The neighbors called them "ham and eggs" because they were always together.

Even on Halloween.

And on the coldest day of winter when everyone else was inside.

One summer Bartholomew taught Nelly to skate by circling his walking stick. "Easy does it!" he warned.

Then she skated right over his toes! He wasn't mad, though. He just whistled and rubbed his foot.

The first time Nelly tried to skate by herself

she fell.

Bartholomew saw that she felt like crying. He pulled up something from the garden and said, "Don't be saddish, have a radish!"

Nelly laughed and ate it. She didn't really like radishes, but she did like Bartholomew.

Before long, Nelly was in school

and Bartholomew had
gotten even older.

Sometimes he needed a helping hand, but he didn't like to take one.

So Nelly held out her hand only when Bartholomew really needed it.

Whenever Bartholomew
had to stop and rest,
Nelly would beg for a
story about the "old days."

Once after a story, she
asked him, "Will we
ever run out of things
to talk about?"

"If we do," said Bartholomew,
"we just won't say anything.
Good friends can do that."

Some days they just took it easy
and sat on the porch.
Bartholomew would play a tune
on his harmonica.
Nelly would make up the words.

One day Bartholomew went out alone
and fell down the stairs. An ambulance
with a red flasher and a siren took him
to the hospital.

He was gone for a long time.

Nelly wrote him every day.
She always ended with
"Come back soon,
so we can go for walks again."

When Bartholomew came home,
he was in a wheelchair.
The smile was gone from his eyes.
"I guess our walks are over," he said.
"No they aren't," said Nelly.
"I can take *you* for walks now."

She knew just how to do it, too.

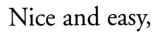
Nice and easy,

not too fast.

Just before Mr. Oliver's
driveway, she would call,
"Get ready for the bump!"

And Bartholomew would wave his hat like a cowboy
as he rode over it.

If they saw a nice dog,
they'd stop and pet it.

But if it was mean, Nelly would shoo it away.

One day when the sprinkler
was on, Nelly started to go
around. But she changed her mind.
"All right, Bartholomew. Ready, set, one, two, three.
CHAAARRRRRRRRRRRRRGE!" And she pushed him
right through it!

124

"Ah…that was fun!" said Bartholomew.

Nelly grinned, "I hope your wheelchair won't rust."

"Fiddlesticks!" He laughed. "Who cares if it does!"

Mrs. Pringle leaned over the fence.
"Seems just like yesterday Bartholomew
was pushing *you* in the stroller."

"That was when I was little,"
said Nelly. "Now it's my turn to
push and Bartholomew's turn to sit…
kind of like a trade."

Then they sat in the sun to dry.
Nelly munched on a carrot.
Bartholomew played a tune on his harmonica.
Nelly could see the old smile was back
in Bartholomew's eyes.

A Special Visit

These first graders visit a special lady. She's like a grandmother to them. She lives in a nursing home. The children like visiting her because they tell her stories.

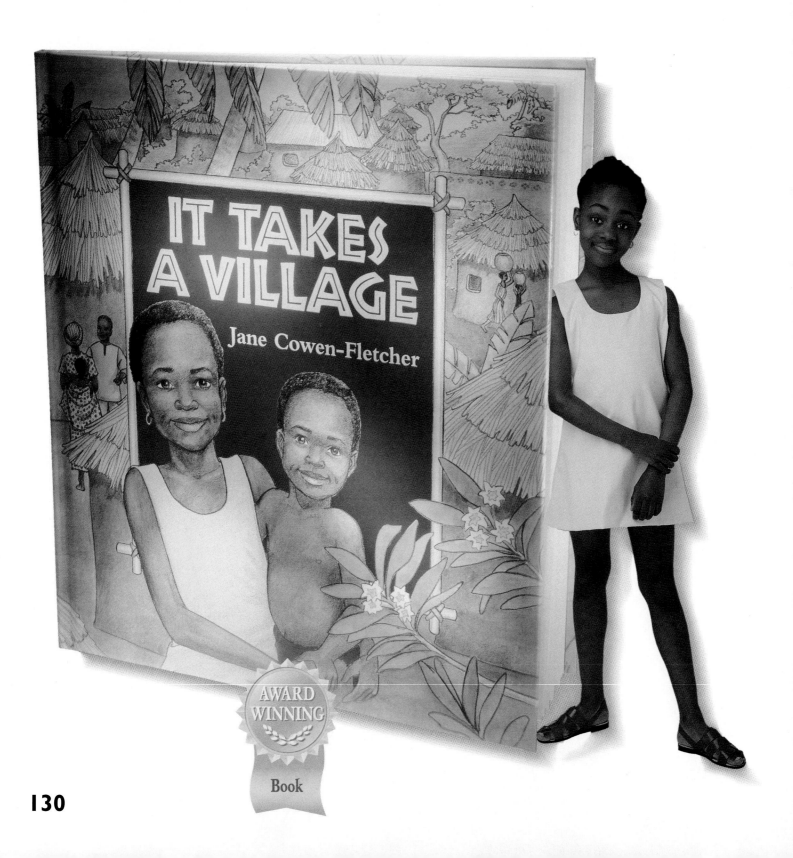

IT TAKES
A VILLAGE

Jane Cowen-Fletcher

AWARD
WINNING

Book

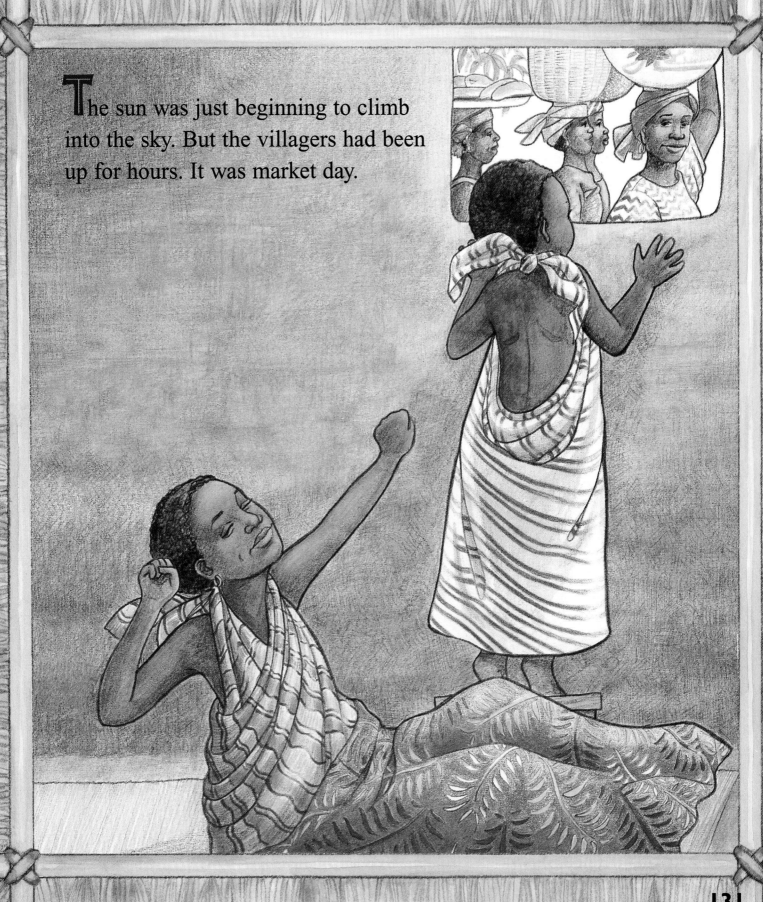

The sun was just beginning to climb into the sky. But the villagers had been up for hours. It was market day.

"Yemi," Mama said, "you must take care of your little brother today while we're at the market. I will be too busy selling our mangoes."

"Come, Kokou," Yemi said, "I will watch you today, all by myself!"

"All by yourself?" Mama asked, and smiled at what Yemi said. Mama knew better.

Mama picked up their mangoes. Yemi picked up Kokou. She felt very grown-up as she walked out of the family compound beside Mama.

They joined the stream of people walking into the village.
People came from all around to sell their goods and buy
whatever they needed. Market day was also a time for visiting.

The greetings started the moment
they stepped on the paths into town.
"Hello!"
"How are you?"
"How is your family?"

Yemi helped Mama set out their mangoes. One of the other fruit vendors said, "Yemi is a big girl now. She is a lot of help to you!"

"Yes," said Mama, "she is going to watch Kokou for me today."

"All by myself," Yemi added.

"All by yourself? *Yay gay!*" the women marveled. They smiled and nodded, but they knew better, too.

When the mangoes were all in neat piles, Yemi asked if she and Kokou could take a look around the market. Mama said, "Yes, but don't be gone too long."

Yemi had not walked very far when Kokou became restless. "He must be hungry," she said. She set him down for just one minute so she could buy some peanuts . . .

. . . and Kokou wandered off.

"*Cho*!" Yemi cried when she turned around and discovered Kokou was gone. She put the peanuts in her pocket . . .

. . . and she hurried off to find him.

"Where could he have gone?" she said.
As Yemi searched for him, she began to worry.
"Kokou must be hungry."

But he was not.

"Kokou must be thirsty."

But he was not.

"Kokou must be frightened."

But he was not.

"Kokou must be hot."

But he was not.

"Kokou must be tired."

But he was not.

Finally, after searching for him everywhere,
Yemi stopped and cried aloud, "Kokou must be lost!"

But he was not.
Just across the path from
where Yemi stood, Kokou was
waking up.
"Is this your Kokou?" the
mat vendor asked.

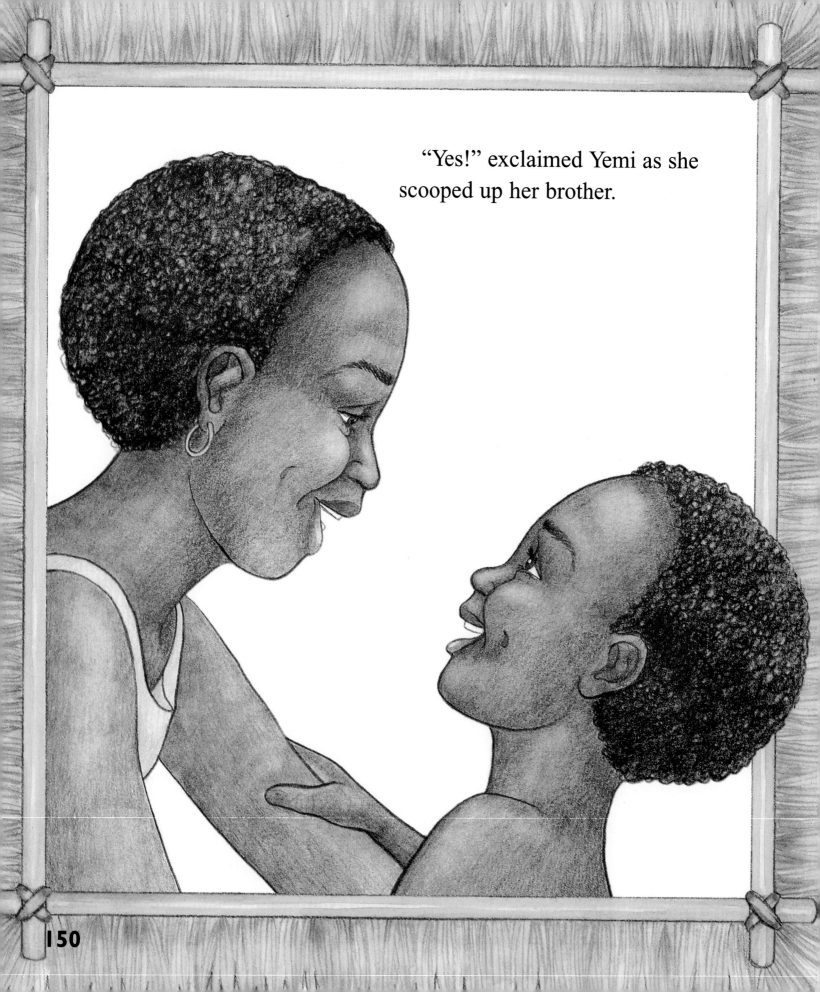

"Yes!" exclaimed Yemi as she scooped up her brother.

"Thank you so much
for taking care of him,"
Yemi said to the mat vendor.

"Oh," he chuckled, "I
was not the only one." He
pointed to where Kokou
had come from.

Yemi thanked him again
and headed off in that
direction.

She said, "Thank you," again . . .

and again . . .

and again . . .

and again.

"We've been gone a long time, Kokou,"
Yemi said. "Mama must be worried."

But she was not. Mama knew better. "As my mama told me, and her mama told her, I will tell you. You weren't alone today, Yemi. We don't raise our children by ourselves. 'It takes a village to raise a child.'"

Glossary

above
over, or in a higher place than, something else
The birds flew **above** the trees.

adults
people who are grown-up
Most **adults** can drive cars.

below
under, or in a lower place than, something else
Mario hung his picture **below** mine.

between
in the middle of two other things
I sat **between** Andy and Connie in the car.

collar
a strap worn around an animal's neck
My dog's **collar** has his name on it.

family
a group of people who are related to and care for one another
A **family** is often made up of a mother, a father, and their children.

harmonica
a small instrument that can be played by blowing air in and out of it
It takes practice to become a good **harmonica** player.

harmonica

hospital
a place where people who are sick or hurt go to get better
I went to the **hospital** to visit my mother.

laughed
to make sounds with the voice to show that something is funny

I **laughed** when I went to the park.

neighbor
someone who lives near you

Our **neighbor** is very friendly.

share
to use with others

We **share** crayons so we all can use many colors.

shelter
something that covers and protects

A house is one kind of **shelter**.

shouted
spoke in a very loud voice

Jenny **shouted** so I would hear her.

sneezed
blew air out of the mouth and nose in a loud way

When Grandpa **sneezed**, everyone said, "Bless you."

special
important and different from all the others

My birthday is a **special** day.

thirsty
a dry feeling you get in your throat when you want something to drink

I was **thirsty** after I ran two miles.

tomorrow
the day after today

If today is Monday, then **tomorrow** is Tuesday.

travelers
people who go from one place to another

Most **travelers** know how much to pack for a trip.

village
a very small place where people live together

A **village** is smaller than a town.

village

Authors and Illustrators

Jane Cowen-Fletcher
pages 130-155

Jane Cowen-Fletcher lived in Benin, West Africa for two years. While there, she sometimes drew pictures of the people she met. She also heard a popular saying that gave her an idea for a children's book. That saying is "It takes a village to raise a child."

Cynthia Rylant   pages 58-73

As a child, Cynthia Rylant grew up in West Virginia. She was always busy playing different kinds of games. She says, "Playing is the greatest training you can have for being a writer. It helps you cook up interesting ideas in your head."

The Relatives Came and *When I Was Young in the Mountains* are just two of the books she has written.

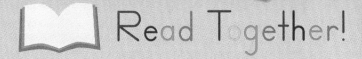 Read Together!

Mamoru Suzuki pages 10-41

Mamoru Suzuki took special care when she painted the pictures for *The Park Bench*. She wanted to give readers clues to how time was passing during the day. If you look very carefully at the pictures in this story, you can tell what time of day it is.

Sally Wittman pages 100-128

Sally Wittman says that people often ask her if *A Special Trade* is a true story. It isn't. But her memories of her own loving grandfather helped her to create the character of Bartholomew.

Almost all of the books Sally Wittman has written tell about friendship. *Pelly and Peak* is a funny book she wrote about two good friends.

Acknowledgments

Grateful acknowledgment is made to the following sources for permission to reprint from previously published material. The publisher has made diligent efforts to trace the ownership of all copyrighted material in this volume and believes that all necessary permissions have been secured. If any errors or omissions have inadvertently been made, proper corrections will gladly be made in future editions.

Cover: Leo Manahan.

Interior: "The Park Bench" from THE PARK BENCH by Fumiko Takeshita, illustrated by Mamoru Suzuki, translated by Ruth A. Kanagy. Copyright © Fumiko Takeshita/Mamoru Suzuki. American text copyright © 1988 by Kane/Miller Book Publishers. Reprinted by permission of Kane/Miller Book Publishers.

Selection and cover from AROUND AND ABOUT MAPS AND JOURNEYS by Kate Petty and Jakki Wood. Copyright © 1993 by Aladdin Books, Ltd. Designed and produced by Aladdin Books Ltd., London. Published by Barron's Educational Series, Inc., Hauppauge, NY. Reprinted by permission.

"The World's a Playground" from *Kid City Magazine*, June 1993. Copyright © 1993 Children's Television Workshop (New York, NY). All rights reserved.

"The Snow Glory" and cover from HENRY AND MUDGE IN PUDDLE TROUBLE by Cynthia Rylant, illustrated by Suçie Stevenson. Text copyright © 1987 by Cynthia Rylant. Illustrations copyright © 1987 by Suçie Stevenson. This edition is reprinted by arrangement with Simon & Schuster Books for Young Readers, Simon & Schuster Children's Publishing Division.

STONE SOUP by Adrienne Betz, illustrated by John O'Brien. Copyright © 1996 by Scholastic Inc.

"A Special Trade" from A SPECIAL TRADE by Sally Wittman, illustrated by Karen Gundersheimer. Text copyright © 1978 by Sally Christensen Wittman. Illustrations copyright © 1978 by Karen Gundersheimer. Reprinted by permission of HarperCollins Publishers.

"It Takes a Village" from IT TAKES A VILLAGE by Jane Cowen-Fletcher. Copyright © 1994 by Jane Cowen-Fletcher. Reprinted by permission.

Cover from FOX ON WHEELS by Edward Marshall, illustrated by James Marshall. Illustration copyright © 1983 by James Marshall. Published by Dial Books for Young Readers, a division of Penguin Books USA Inc.

Cover from THE LEAVING MORNING by Angela Johnson, illustrated by David Soman. Illustration copyright © 1992 by David Soman. Published by Orchard Books.

Cover from MARGARET AND MARGARITA, MARGARITA Y MARGARET by Lynn Reiser. Illustration copyright © 1993 by Lynn Whisnant Reiser. Published by William Morrow & Company, Inc.

Cover from MICHAEL BIRD-BOY by Tomie dePaola. Illustration copyright © 1975 by Tomie dePaola. Published by Simon & Schuster Books for Young Readers, Simon & Schuster Children's Publishing Division.

Cover from THE WAY TO CAPTAIN YANKEE'S by Anne Rockwell. Illustration copyright © 1994 by Anne Rockwell. Published by Simon & Schuster Books for Young Readers, Simon & Schuster Children's Publishing Division.

Photography and Illustration Credits

Selection Opener Photographs by David S. Waitz Photography/Alleycat Design, Inc.

Photos: p. 2 tl: © Joe Carini for Scholastic Inc.; br: © Kyle Rothenborg/Pacific Stock; tr: © Rita Ariyoshi/Pacific Stock; bl: © David Cornwell/Pacific Stock; bc: © Reggie David/Pacific Stock. p. 3 br: © Joe Carini for Scholastic Inc.; bl: © Greg Vaughn/Pacific Stock; tl: © Greg Vaughn/Pacific Stock. p. 42 cl, bl: © Joe Carini for Scholastic Inc. p. 43 c: © Joe Carini for Scholastic Inc. p. 129 bl, br: © Stephen Ogilvy for Scholastic Inc.; tl: © David Lawrence for Scholastic Inc.; picture frame: © Stephen Ogilvy for Scholastic Inc. p. 156 cr: © Stephen Ogilvy for Scholastic Inc. p. 157 br: © Erik Leigh Simmons/The Image Bank. p. 158 br: © Courtesy of Scholastic Trade Department; bl: Priya Nair.

Illustrations: pp. 2-3: Jackie Snider; pp. 8-9, 56-57: Jim Owens; pp. 74-75: David Slonim; pp. 76-97: John O'Brian; pp. 98-99: Jim Owens; pp. 130-155: Jane Cowen-Fletcher.